If I Had Longer Legs I'd Be a Giant

If I Had Longer Legs I'd Be a Giant

Written and Illustrated by

John Wesley Burton

A Cavalletto Press Book
Cavalletto Press, Morehead, Ky

ISBN: 9798603799780

Contents

Introductions

CROW

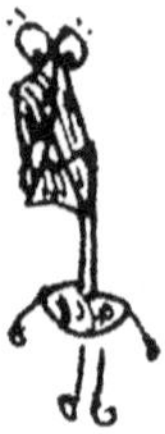

TURTLE

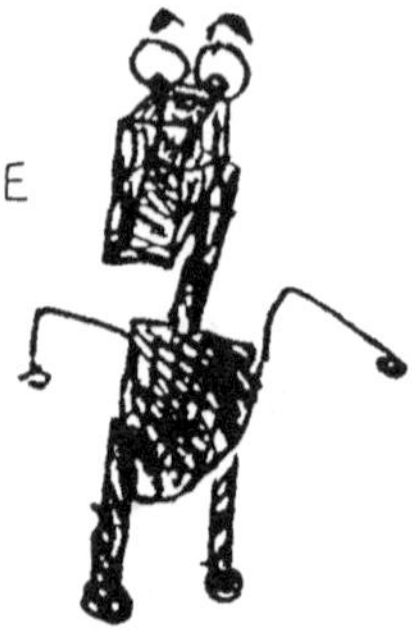

BOY SCOUT

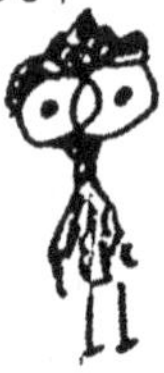

SPACE DOG

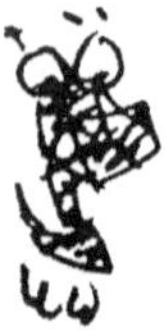

DOLLAR

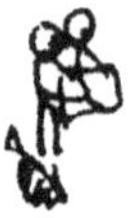

LIGHT BULB

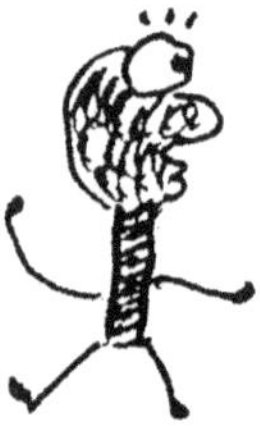

JUNEBUG

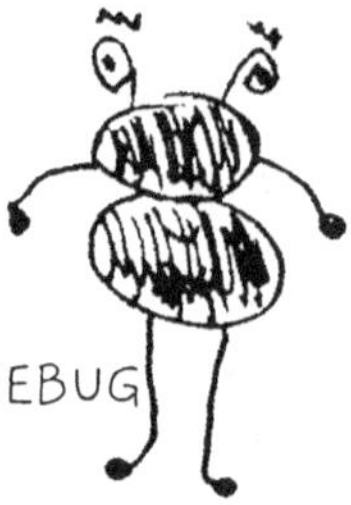

WHITE OAK

BIRDIE

BRIGHT LIGHT

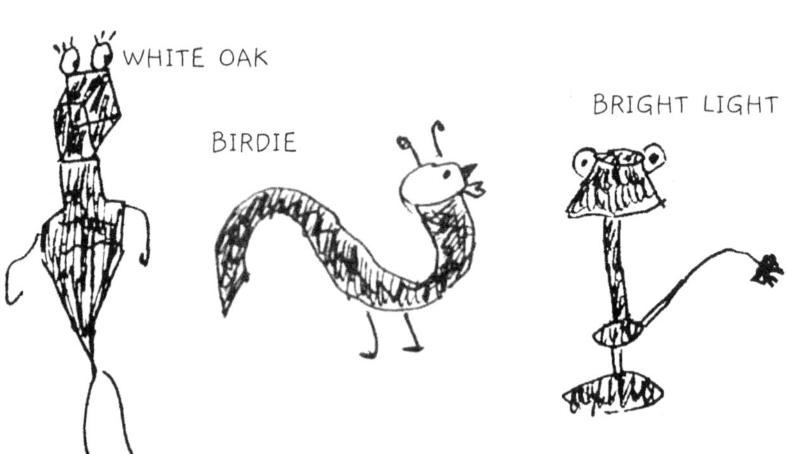

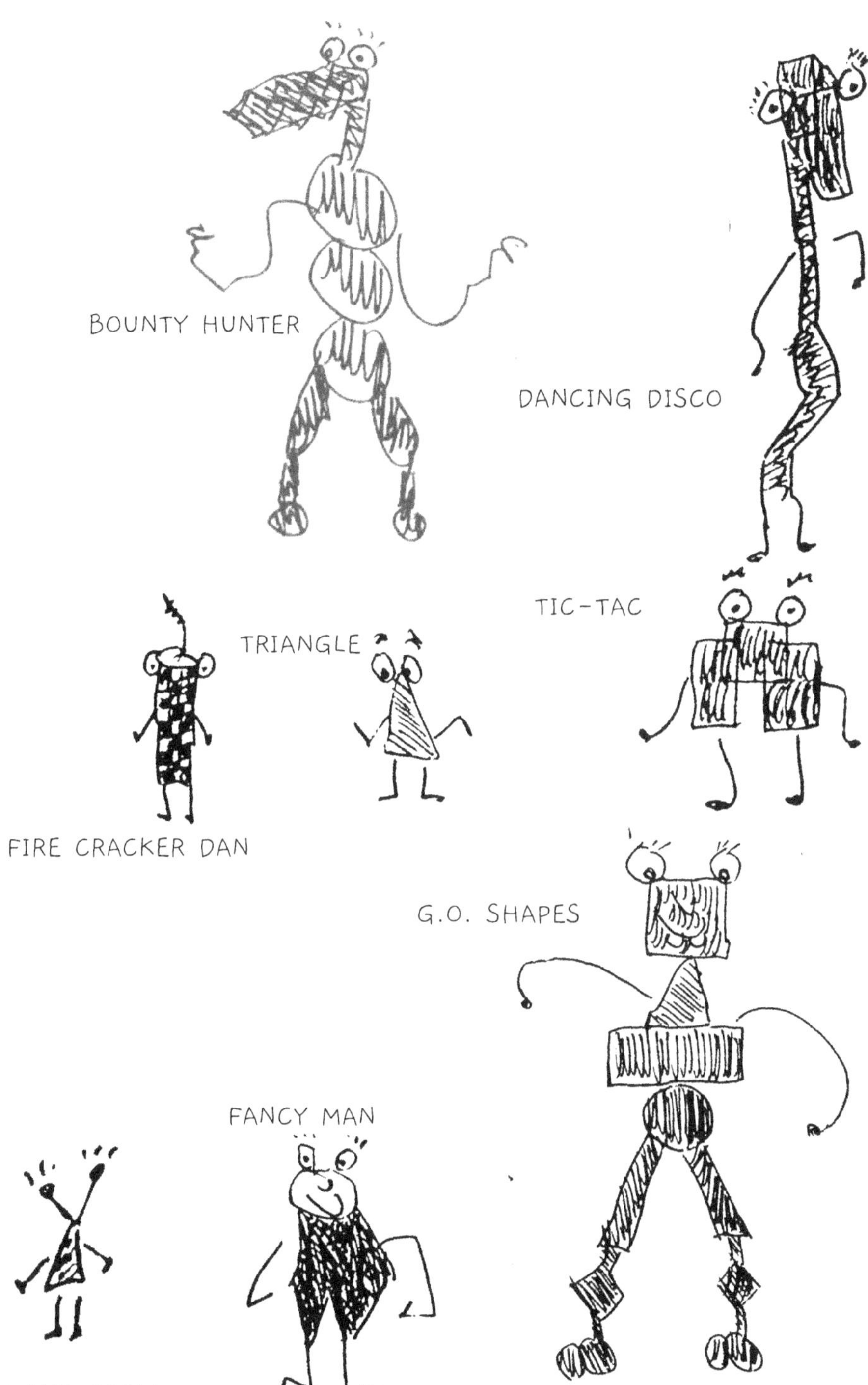

BOUNTY HUNTER
DANCING DISCO
TRIANGLE
TIC-TAC
FIRE CRACKER DAN
G.O. SHAPES
FANCY MAN
WHIP CREAM

A Soldier's Gift

A Holy Bible
Containing the written
Books of Moses
Being his first
Book Genesis
Extremely small type
Published 1854
Mother Sent
It to her
Son Thomas
Thomas could be
Only a single
Name of a man
Of color
Or Thomas
Could be a last
Name of any
Civil War soldier
It travelled
Through our war
Torn lands
To a command post
And from there to
A mother's son
To the soldier's hands
Words scribed within
This Holy Bible
On the first
Clear page
Are words that were
Possibly written
By the captured
Soldier himself
There were thousands
Of Confederate Soldiers

Captured at Fort Donelson
February 15, 1862
Abraham Lincoln President
Ulysses S. Grant Union General
Who got the surrendering
Of the Confederate Army there
Today there is no
Historical information
Of what became
Of Mom's son
The soldier
The prisoner
Of the Civil War
1861 through 1865
What we know is
The historical fact
That the Hand Bible
Did survive
The Civil War
We don't know
How this Bible
Travelled back
Across the lands
Of reconstruction
His mother is gone
Her son Thomas
The soldier is gone
We don't know
How he went
As prisoner of war
Or a freed man
This Holy Bible
Survived through
A lot of war
By leaving mother's house
Traveling directly through
The destruction

Of this war
Did it ever
Reach the hands
Of Thomas
The soldier
Captured at prison camp
There is no historical
Information
Of where this Holy Bible's
Journey began
Think about it
For a few minutes
Published 1854
The year is now 2019
165 years has passed
With this Small Hand Bible
Remaining in existence
The same Holy Bible
A mom
Sent her son
A Civil War Soldier
Of 1861-1865
History will remember
That Mother's
Little Hand Bible
Will keep its
Historical journey sealed
A part of Civil War history
Was going to become
Strings of paper
Through the recycling process
The Small Hand Holy Bible
Mom's gift
To her son Thomas
A Civil War Soldier
Captured at Fort Donelson
Many years ago

A son
A soldier
A prisoner of war
A person
Of color or white
Would have been
Forgotten
It was a second
Miracle
That the Small
Holy Bible
Was spared
And had the opportunity
To share with
Us historically
That this Holy Bible
Was in the hands
Of a mother's son
A soldier
A prisoner during
The Civil War
Of 1861 - 1865

A Visit from St. Crow

Twas the night before Christmas
When all through the woods
There was a creature stirring
It wasn't a mouse
It was the queen of the sky
A crow black as night
Even this wonderful bird
Had a stocking hung
By the Chimney with care
In hope that St. Crow
Would soon be there
All of the other
Young birdies
Nested and all
Snug in their beds
Visions of gold and silver coins
Dancing within their heads
Mamma bird
The queen of queens
Standing in front of the fireplace
Wearing her beautiful
Red cap
All of we birds
Relaxed our brains
And were desperately
Wanting to rest
A long time during
Winters grasp
Suddenly out on the lawn
Appeared St. Crow
With his magical feathers
I sprang from my winters nap
To see what was going on
Away to the window
I flew like a dash

Opened up the curtain
And I suddenly saw
The picture
That was before my eyes
Was natures art
The moon was sparkling
In the sky
As if it were
A golden coin
Oh there on the ground
Was a silvery
New fallen snow
The minerals
That my wondering
Eyes did want to see
A miniature sleigh
And eight tiny crows
With St. Crow
Being the older driver
So lively and feathered
I knew within
That moment
That it was St. Crow
More rapid than eagles
His coursers they came
He whistled and shouted
Called them by name
Now Hatchett
Now Pioneer
Now Prancer and White Oak
On Reece Cup
On Rookie
On Milk Dud and Mountain News
To the top
Of the porch
To the highest part
Of the wall

Now fly away
Fly away all
As leaves would leave the Hickory
Before the wild hurricane
Would have had a chance to fly
They met an obstacle
Mounted within the sky
Up to the housetop
The coursers they flew
With the sleigh
Full of gold and silver
And St. Crow too
Did they now
In a twinkling
Of a moment
I heard on the roof
The flapping
Of each little pair of wings
As I drew in my head
And was turning around
Down the chimney St. Crow
Came with a flop
He was dressed
All in feathers
From his head to his feet
His clothes were all
The darkest black could be
A bundle of gold and silver
He had flung on his back
And he looked like
A client going to the bank
His eyes
How happily they appeared
His dimples
I didn't vision at all
His beak
Was straight as an arrow

And his mouth
Was shaped that of a bow
He appeared
To be a beardless crow
Therefore
He had no beard
As white as snow
The stump of a pipe
He held tight in his beak
The smoke
It encircled his head
like a string
Of Christmas lights
He had a rather handsome face
And a little round belly
That shook
When he sung his music
Like a bowl
Full of jello
He was chubby and plump
A right jolly old bird
And I laughed
When I saw him
In spite of myself
A wink
Of one of his eyes
And a twist
Of his head
And then a wink
From the other eye
Had given me to know
I had nothing to dread
He sung his music
With not a word
But continued his work
And filled
All the little birdies stockings

Then turned
Like an airplane
Ready for flight
He placed his finger
Aside of his beak
And giving a nod
Up the chimney
He flew
He was back
In his sleigh
With his team
He gave a whistle
Away they all flew
Like shooting stars
I heard
Him and his team say
Before they were
Out of sight
To all a good night

Years Taking Flight

The Library
Was my second home
For many years

For those people who knew me
During my elementary
And high school days

Have somewhat remembered
A personality which always
Remained the same no matter what

How the years have taken flight
And now the wings of the eagle
Seem to be flapping again

A bundle
Of joy
My baby boy

Some say that my smile
Appears to be as sweet
As honey on a blueberry bush

As the Lord is My Shepherd
I will walk through
The valley of retirement

Parties do begin and end
I will miss all who have
Followed me down this road

Even though the storms
Were rain sometimes
And other storms were snow

Life is a journey
It is time for me
To make a u-turn

And begin the
Next part of my journey
For who knows where

The Mountains and My Hometown

Ozzie said it best
You will be working
In the Learning Resource Center
He knew it before me
But you are the greatest
His words of wisdom
A proven fact
Shooting muskets a sport
Arrows shot from a distance
Center of the Bulls Eye
Without a doubt
Throwing the tomahawk
At a homemade target
Bulls Eye solid red
No escape from my
Tomahawk throw
Rattle snakes living
In the mountains
Come down to my home
Most of the time
I send them on their way
Back up to the high lands
Daniel Boone born
November 02
Several years before
I was born
On the same month and day
I have no trouble
Driving through the mountains
Covered with ice and snow
A young lady
With the knowledge of Chemistry
To be a pharmacist
Is a career goal
I am not a talker

But within the Learning Resource Center
I am a great communicator
With strings of words
And sentences of many
Therefore I am a person
Who talks to some degree
But not to everyone
A person who fears spiders
But an artist
Somewhat like her grandmother
Drawn the most perfect spider
For an art contest during Halloween
Turkey drawing contest
Won the last two
Loves to eat chocolate
And drank ALE 8 and tea
Wants to go to Ireland
And visit her kin
Artist of Red Bear
Friend of Black Bear
Two of her most liked sayings
The haymaker 360
I have not a lot of money
So I have to pay you in marbles
The most I like of all
Is to go with my father
On a wilderness sporting event
Drawings can be drawn
Arrows can be shot from a bow
The tomahawk can be thrown
The haymaker 360
Can outdo them all
A friend indeed
Sandy from the same
Mountains as me
The land close to higher mountains
Will always be my home

There is much more
That could be said
But I am now in my hometown
Working for summer wages
That I will need
For my economic road ahead

Blackberry Pie Time Again

As the music begins to play
It is just another day
When will the blackberries
On the needle bushes be ripe again
The snows this winter
Were somewhat
Non occurring this December
It is blackberry pickin time again
Early July is finally here
The beautiful blackberries
Leave the thorn bush
They are put in a freezer
And then into the pie pan
With jumble bells
And open wells
Become Hickory trees
Yesterday's blackberries
It is blackberry pie time again
How tasty
With milk and sugar
The storm is upon
The mountain today
It is blackberry pie time again
Little ones small and green
Appalachian hills in Hazard
Rolling as they do
The one room school
Was named after the song or poem
It is blackberry pie time again
This song holds a special magic
A musical sound of the dulcimer
Appalachian music can be heard
In the pie pan as the blackberry pie bakes
A beautiful sound
The color of winters frost

It is a language of a different dialect
That makes the blackberries speak
While they become
Blackberry pie time again

The World of Volleyball

Here it is Thursday evening
Another day's work had past
Who were library employees earlier today
Transformed themselves
Into construction workers

Finally
The volleyball net is up
Time to serve
Ray is on the move

Bonita stands behind the blue line
She swings her powerful right hand
Hits the volleyball
It is traveling at the speed of light

Finds Ray
He double clutches
With a spontaneous hit
That drives the ball directly into the net

Stephanie always plays
On the side of her friend
She shouts positive cheers of happiness
As the server gets another point
Against the mighty Power Ranger Coach Ray

Tom
A coach also
Bonita
A member of his team

Quentin is standing firmly in his spot
Here it comes
Bonita's
Serve again

As Ray
Had attempted earlier
Quentin hit the volleyball
Directly out of bounce

Barry
Turns to his teammates
And
Gives a thumbs up

Rhonda
Loves to see Ray
Dance nervously on the volleyball court
She gives the audience a great big smile

After Bonita
Had scored
Another point
Against Ray's team

Jason
Where is he
A trip
To Virginia

He told me before he went on his trip
To watch Bonita
She scored nine straight points
When serving the volleyball
During the final game last Thursday night

Chris B.
Hit a serve delivered from Bonita
The volleyball went the whole length
of the court and then some
Donna was standing anxiously
Wanting to hit the volleyball
That will be served by Bonita

She could have an opportunity
To change server position
This didn't happen

She returned
The volleyball back over the volleyball net
But there had been several exchanges
During this event
Bonita scores another point

Kevin enters
The game late
Who's ahead says he
He gets the response
And joins the winning team

Suddenly
There is some disagreement
On the volleyball floor
Bonita doesn't hear the disturbance

Assistant Coach Lisa
Keeps her eyes
Focused on the server
Hoping the volleyball
Will try to cross her path

Bonita delivers her volleyball serve
Directly to Quentin
He hooks the volleyball
A downward rocket drive
Straight to Stephanie

Is was about time
The serve has changed course
Laura has an opportunity
To score for Ray's team

Her serve
Was short-lived
She hits the volleyball
A ninety-degree line drive right into the net

Stephanie
Is serving
The volleyball now
She hits a great serve

Chris M.
Hits the volleyball straight to Bonita
As she did when she served the volleyball
Another good hit

John
Was playing all the positions on the court
And missed his opportunity
To return the volleyball to the other side
Another point scored for Tom's team

Ray must have a time out
What can he tell his team
That will turn
The tide the other way

A couple minutes had past
Ray whistles for a time out
His team huddles around him as he talks
Fiercely with a lecture well delivered

Tom's team started to go downhill
The powerhouse sever
Couldn't buy a point from his serve

Finally Ray scored a point off his serve
He couldn't be stopped
He served the volleyball
Three times in a row

Coach Ray's time out message
Must have expired
His team started to sleep on the court
It was Bonita again
They feared her serve

Tom
Needed no time out
His team
Was here tonight to win

Ray timed out
A second time
While walking back to the court
With his team following him

He glanced at the time
Displayed on the face of his watch
And told us it was about time
To take the volleyball net down

Tom's team
With Bonita chosen the most valuable player
Was ahead of Ray's team
By 14 points

It was hard to convince Bonita
To honor the string of words that Ray
Uttered rather harshly
These words being

The team that gets the next
Point wins the game
We will see all of you
On the volleyball
Court again someday

— 24 —

Dressed as Goblins

Pumpkins lay
Sleeping under weeds
In the garden
Not seeing
The tomatoes getting
Bit by October frost
Scarecrows dance
With golden corn stalks
That remain
In the soil
Plastic ghosts stand
On weather-beaten porches
Cars, trucks, and motorcycles
Bring goblins
To our community
How they
Do scare us folks
When they come
As such
Even the friendly ghost
Would have been scared
During this event
Monstrous hands
Reach towards
Large bowls
Of popcorn balls
Who are
These creatures
From who
Knows where
English
They had mastered
The words
They had to say
Were trick-or-treat

A treat
They received
And then
Were on their way
To scare
Another family
Who lives
Farther down
This dirt road
Halloween goblins
Come and go
Quickly
They have only
Two hours
To complete
Their evening
Event
Home is now
Where they
Are at
Observing
All the treats
They had received
This trick-or-treat
Halloween night

Joretta Gay Pugh's
(Heavenly Call)

Before GOD heard my call
My righteousness was lost
Mercy on me he had none
I wanted him to hear my prayer
I was laying down in pain and sleep
I was wanting to get all of my trust in him
Lest I would sleep the sleep of pain
Didn't eat didn't drink
For several days
Weaker and weaker I became
My walking alone came to none
My mind was still sharp and clear
Peace was plentiful
When GOD heard my call
It is GOD who made
My way perfect
After my final minutes of suffering
I went to sleep
The pain I had in my body
For the last three years
I will have no more
I am in heaven now
For GOD answered my call

A Little Girl
(All Grown up)

You tell
Me to grow up
Well let's
Compare scars
Give me
One minute
And I'll show
You my heart
You tell me
 I smile
 Like I've never
 Been hurt
That is simply
Because
I've already
Learned that
Big girls
Cry alone
Where no one
Can see
With only
Their cover
To give them
The comfort
They need
Because people
Can be heartless
And people
Can be mean
And crying
With an audience
Is admitting
That you are weak
And let us face

Some facts
No one really
Cares
Crying in front
Of an audience
Is just accepting
Blank stares
And being
Rejected
Is always easier
At night
When no one is
Around
To come hold
Me tight
Because
Even if they
Were there
Comfort you would
Never find
Because just
Like the rest
They would say
Big girls don't cry
Well momma
Here I am
Can't you hear
Me crying
Can't you look
Up from yourself
And see
That I am dying
All I ever
Wanted
Was for you
To love me
Even when

I am weak
Don't let
Me be lonely
Momma
Don't you see me
You told me
I would always
Be your little girl
So momma
Why did
You hurt me
And then
Leave me
To this world
I can remember
I can count
On one hand
Every time
You chose me
Every time
For me
You made a stand
But mom
I can't count
How many times
You left me
For them
How many times
You had chosen
The sex
The drugs
The men
And mommy
I am just like you
Aren't you
So proud
I'm heartless and cold

I'm obnoxious and loud
And every single day
I try to escape
This burning
Need to cry
This emptiness inside
Momma
Aren't you so proud
Momma
I'm all grown up
Momma
I hate myself
Because I
Never earned
Your love
Momma
I hate myself
Because
I was never enough
Momma I take
All of this aggression
Out on men
Momma
The never
Ending cycle
Starts again
Momma
Do you love me
Now
Because momma
They say love
And I say how

Halloween Night All Over Again

At the end of the year
Comes turkey and St. Nick
But before these two things
Are the Halloween frights
Only once in a year
A few times in your life
Scaring the life out of people
Is what it is about
Getting chocolates and caramels
By the dozens and pounds
Makes each hallowed nightfall
Expected each year
A day of excitement
When it finally comes around
Dressed in costumes galore
The vampires and clowns
Come knocking each year
On everyone's door
Asking for goodies
Is not the proper way
Ringing the doorbell
And disappearing
Will gain you the day
You would want to be ruthless
A thing in the night
Just take my advice
Give everyone a scare
On this Halloween Night

Hard Times

I've lived
Through hard times
I had not a nickel
Nor a dime
I dug into
My pockets
Both wells were dry
No coins for a coke
To buy
From the machine outside
This was the times
Of the Great Depression

Price of Crude

The pump
Out of Order
Price
A chilling cost
Cash only
Visa check cards
Not accepted
A cheaper grade
Corn made
French fries
And onion rings
Water vapors
Out the tail pipe
Global warming
Slowed somewhat
An engine only
Needs gallons of fuel

Jack and the Candlestick

Jack was nimble
Oh yeal
He was quick
His Visa Check Card
Would not click
How poor was he
So poor
That he could not
Buy a candlestick
Therefore
He did not
Make a jump

Olden Tymes Christmas

Thanksgiving had passed
Let's get a Christmas Tree
The children were pacing back and forth
Pattering circles on the hard dirt floor

Pot- Bellied stove
Singing Silent Night
All was calm
Hickory popping and cracking
In the warm air

The old tymer
Wanting to be heard
Telling his story about a Christmas
From his childhood

Twas a sound of ice pellets
Hitting the wooden-shingled roof
Of our weather-beaten house
While the little ones listened to his words

A small child's voice echoed
Through the warmth of the air
In the direction
Of the old tymers hard-to-hearing ears

What was Christmas like during olden tymes
The old tymer commences to tell his story
That had lived in his long-term memory
About a Christmas a long tyme ago

His voice quivered as he spoke
Olden tyme Christmas
Wasn't as we know Christmas today
Even the Christmas Tree was real

A voice shouted from a distance
Among the audience
How did we come to have a Christmas Tree
The Christmas Tree was special

We took a doubled-bladed axe
And searched many hours
We cut down the most beautiful
Christmas Tree
From the harsh winter floor

From the mountainous point
We drug it home
During the long haul
We had to pause to catch our breath

Our chosen Christmas Tree
Wasn't artificial like
The evergreen trees on display
Standing on tables
At Wal-Mart stores throughout the world

Why
A voice rang out from the audience
The Christmas Tree we had cut down
Was beyond perfect
Magic appeared in its needles

We counted five needles
On a single cluster
Therefore we knew
It was the Magical White Pine

The magic
Wasn't in the Pine
But in its first name White
Meaning a spiritual Christmas

White Christmas
Is what we dreamed about
The spirit white always brought
December 25 alive

We put this magical Christmas Tree
In the only room
We had in our
Weather-beaten home

All of us children
Knew
That this perfect Christmas Tree
Was magical

The corn we popped
In an iron pot
With a lid
Covering the top

The pot-bellied stove
Was working overtime
To make the spiritual pops
Of puffy white popcorn

This becoming most beautiful
After it had been strung
Through a needle
At the end of a white piece of thread

The magical Christmas Tree
That we had decorated
In the only room inside
Our weather-beaten home

Was the magical Christmas Tree
That stood tall and straight
As if it were a soldier
That December day

In front of a window or not
This glorious display
Had became the brightest light
In our weather beaten home

All of us children
Had a Christmas stocking to hang
From a branch
On this breath taking Pine

I was the eldest child
Me being 9 years old
The youngest child
Only 2 years old

The oil-lamp usually burned
A dim light
That had been used for
Reading purposes only

But during this tyme of year
It fed light
To the white
Fluffy strings of popcorn

The reflected light
From each piece of popcorn
Had become the color spectrum

That the heavenly artist used to paint a rainbow
During an early summer rainstorm on a sun-shining day

These magnificent colors
Gave the entire weather beaten home
What it took
To make the Christmas Tree
Magic come to life

Take a minute and imagine
How beautiful
Our perfect
Christmas Tree had become

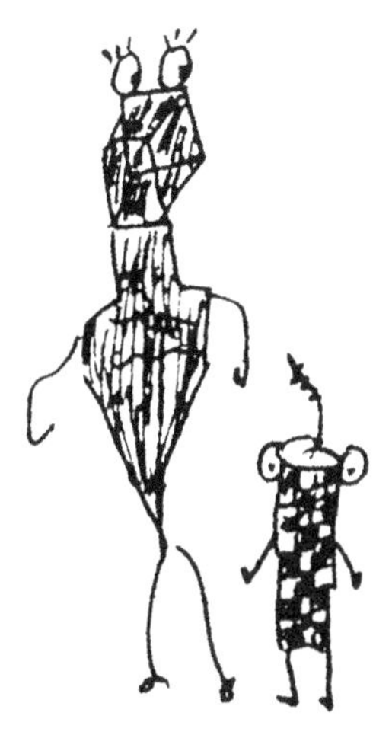

With its beautiful green needles
White strings of white puffy popcorn
And the beautiful
Reflection from rainbow colored
Non-electric lights

Mother and father would sit
Close to the pot-bellied stove
Lean their cane-bottomed chairs
On their two back legs
And watch the flickering colored popcorn
Lights joyfully light up the room

I the eldest child
Remembered the golden harvest
Of fruit
This past Summer

Our bright red Christmas stockings
With white bands
Laced around them
Hung down and touched the hard dirt floor

The tyme had arrived
It was Christmas Eve
Early to bed early to rise
Santa and Friendly Freddie
His elf would be here soon

He would arrive from the sky
Riding in a huge sleigh
Pulled by nine reindeer
With Friendly Freddie riding beside him

For a whole year
The elves gathered
Apples, oranges, and candy canes
And the reindeer
Would only work pulling
The sleigh for one night

I remember as it were yesterday
Pa had a sleigh
That was pulled by our two mules
Hay Patch and Four-Leaf-Clover

This sleigh of ours
Never pulled Christmas gifts
It was used
For pulling chores and going to church
Come Sunday morning

Let me say
Nothing more
About the two
Sleighs

Christmas day is tomorrow
After going to bed
To get a good nights rest
Sleeping on my duck-feathered mattress

I couldn't sleep
My mind wondering
What would Santa's gift
Be for a 9 year old boy

Remember
I am the eldest son
I removed my Christmas stocking
From the magical Christmas Tree

In my stocking
A block of coal
I was considered an adult
By Santa and his Elf

I was as happy
As two turtle doves singing
Because inside my Christmas stocking
Was a magical white block of coal
Meaning white spirit of Christmas

Santa gave me this message
Because he wanted to make absolutely sure
That I would continue to go
 With my younger brothers and sisters

To the top
Of mountainous wilderness
To locate and cut down
The magical Christmas Tree
For next Christmas

The white block of coal
Had a story to tell
Of a baby boy
Born in Bethlehem
Receiving gifts many years ago

This is the story
You are at the present time the same age
As the Three Kings
And the Little Drummer Boy
Who brought gifts

To the New Born King
The Little ones minds wondered too
For them it had been a long winter's nap
We knew Christmas had arrived
Snow White covered the cold dark ground

The spirit of Christmas was alive everywhere
That Christmas day
Santa and his helper Friendly Freddie
Had visited their home during the night before

The little ones found
An apple, an orange, and a candy cane
In their beautiful
Christmas stocking

I the eldest child
Was happy for them
This being the best
Christmas they had ever had

The Three Kings had given gifts
To baby Jesus
They had no gifts
For themselves

The Little Drummer Boy was poor
But he brought his drums
So he could play them
For the New Born King

The real magic of Christmas
Isn't in the spiritual color white
The magical Christmas Tree
And it is not in the white magical
Block of coal

The real magic of Christmas is the giving of
gifts to the children
Who have not reached their ninth birthday
The three Kings and The Little Drummer
Boy were nine years old
When they gave a gift to the baby Jesus

Santa and Friendly Freddie
Were with The Three Kings
And The Little Drummer Boy
When they were taking their gifts

To the new born king
They asked Santa and Friendly Freddie
To continue
Giving gifts to the children
Who are under the age of nine

The children at the age of nine
Will do as The Three Kings
And The Little Drummer Boy had done
Many years ago
Give a gift to their younger siblings
On Christmas Day

Santa was a jolly man
Dressed in his red suit
Friendly Freddie
Was a tall elf
Even though he was a short
Elf at two-feet-two

Now Santa and Friendly Freddie
Had a secret
That they didn't
Want told

Parents allow your children
Who are at the age of nine
Hang their Christmas stocking
On the perfect magical
Christmas Three

Santa will share his secret himself
Every Christmas Day
Throughout
The history of the Christmas Days
That are yet to come

Every nine year old child
Will have in his/her
Christmas stocking
A white block of coal

Halloween Night

On a spooky
Halloween night
When goblins and witches
Come out to fight
When children go out to say
Trick or Treat
When goblins and witches
And people meet
Around the town
Loud noises roar
When you hear the sound
Of the knocking at your door
Should you open it
Should you be scared
Trick or Treaters are everywhere
But don't you worry
Don't you fright
Its only one day
One evening
It is Halloween Night

Fever on Red River

I didn't know!
My oldest sister, Sarah caught it
While she was washing clothes
On the washboard at our swimming hole
Her hands nearly frozen
From the chill of the water
And the wind screaming rather harshly
As time pushed it up the river
To the top of the mountain

She couldn't carry the frozen clothes
To our little shack
Her frame was too weak
We carried the clothes home that day
And hung them to dry close
To the fireplace in the kitchen
We also told father

That Sarah was deathly sick with fever
Father brought Sarah home on the sled pulled by
our gray mule
This was the last time we had seen her standing
On her own two feet

She then lay in her bedroom
Sweating with fever
While lying upon her cherry bed
The clock hanging on the wall in the kitchen
Appeared to be missing a beat now and then
As her heart was struggling
To make a ticking sound
Seems as if darkness was a long time coming

There were four of us children
Our parents were hurt

Though to them there were no
Physical pain endured
There wasn't anything that they could do
To help their oldest child
Her suffering tremendously with feverish chills
As time sets with her through the daylight hours

I would hear mother and father praying
While they were stuffing the three new pillows
With soft, white duck feathers
That they had picked from our ducks
Before they had a chance to waddle
In the cold muddy water
In the small mudhole close to the barn
I knew it
I had always done my thinking
Through exploration

There was something going on here
Besides stuffing the three new pillows
With soft, white duck feathers
I didn't know why there was a need
To investigate
But time told me not to just sit still

I seen the wooden box
The carpenter had assembled
By using his hammer, nails, and cured White Pine lumber
Also I seen that it was lined
With ticking that had been
Packed with the soft, white duck feathers
This verdict I didn't want to discover
Time was preparing for what was yet to come

The battle was between time and death
We had no answer to which would succeed
Dr. Northcutt had never been invited

To our home before
Especially riding his black horse
Twenty miles through a life threatening
Winter storm

He appeared to be frozen solid
Ice pellets had crystallized
The fingers on his right-hand
Because they were hanging
Out of the holes in his wool glove
The doctor needed help
It was time that had the winter storm
To follow him here

And it was death living within the frozen
Vapors that caused his body to freeze
The doctor stood in front of our small
fireplace in the kitchen
He held his frozen fingers close
To the bluish-red flames
That had been born from the burning of the
Flickering hickory wood

I noticed that his frame
Was nervously shaking
And his fingers starting to tingle
As if the blood circulation
In his right-hand
Had been cut off by frostbite
As the minutes had passed
The doctor was relieved
The winter storm
Had not caused him any loss

I asked myself
What could he do
His left-hand was folded into a fist

While he rapped on Sarah's bedroom
Door softly
Not wanting to disturb his patient
His black medical bag hanging down
From his right-hand
Close to the dirt floor inside of Sarah's
Bedroom

Mom did as the doctor had asked
She continuously went to the well
To draw cold water
So he could keep a cold damp wash cloth
Applied to Sarah's forehead
The cold moisture was suppose
To destroy the fever within her body

He did the best that he could have done
To cure our sister
Yes! He did the best that he could have done
To cure our sister
Time and death are the only two soldiers
That remained in Sarah's battle

The visitor that had entered Sarah's body
Was powerful
The doctor told us he knew the monster
And tried to destroy it a few days ago
The Jacob's only child had the same sickness
The same medical procedures
Had been applied
But there too death had defeated time
Yellow Fever is spreading
Throughout the land

Father walked and paved the dirt floors
In his shack continuously
Always stopping for a second

To glance outside to the top of the mountain
By looking through the small window
On the left wall
Close to the wooden door
Inside the living room

He walked this two-way path
Until his legs began to ache
With tremendous pain
But the pain dealing
With his daughter's health was much worse

Father's memory takes him back in time
As he remembers Sarah
His beautiful daughter
Her golden hair
Hanging mid-way down her back
Lying in curls
A skeleton frame was all that was left

How many hours she had to live
Even time couldn't tell
As the days past
The killer, Yellow Fever had taken its toll
Robbing Sarah's body from its soul
Death was the only soldier
That remained in her bedroom
For time had strayed away

Father told mother
I made a promise to my ten-year-old
Daughter six years ago
Seemed to me that time was talking then
I remember it as if it were yesterday
We were standing, glancing out the window
On the left wall
Beside the wooden door in the living room

These where the words
That my ten-year-old daughter said to me
"Daddy"!
"When I die I want to be buried out there
On the hill
And I want the rest of my family
Up there with me when the Angel of Death
Takes their body from their soul"

Sarah was sixteen years old
When the sickness entered her body
Her golden hair
Hung mid-way down her back
Lying in Curls
Remained beautiful
Time fought a defensive battle
All wasn't gone there was still life

The doctor came to us with the news
That we didn't want broadcasted
But it was as the doctor had reported
Her body lay cold in her bedroom
Upon her cherry bed
Father kept his promise
He had made to his ten-year-old daughter

The doctor also told us
That the burial should be done
As quickly as possible
To keep the monster
From spreading farther up Red River
Taking more innocent people's lives.
Father didn't know
Whether or not his daughter's burial could
Have been classified as a funeral

Sarah's casket
Father had assembled with his own hands
And mother had lined it
With the ticking that she had stuffed
With the soft, white duck feathers
The family carried Sarah in her casket
To the top of the mountain

The doctor attended the burial
Though it was a sad day
He had not brought a cure
To kill the monster
That could be the birth
Of a plague
That would roam
Disastrously through the countryside

Father spoke a few words for his daughter
And eventually bent down
Towards the ground
Picked up his shovel
And commenced to cover his daughter's
Homemade casket
With clay, mud, and rock
He done the best he could have done
Because of the winter storm

Father was the only person
That remained on the mountain
After the burial
The doctor, her siblings, and her mother
Had walked back down the mountain
To the little shack
That stood close to the barn

Every May 30th father, mother and siblings
Go to the top of the mountain

And put Real Bright Red Roses
On Sarah's grave
They remember the beautiful girl
With her golden hair
Hanging mid-way down her back
Lying in curls

Pluto's Aliens
(So far Away from Earth)

Space the final destiny of the alien species
Creatures green with lightbulb heads
They came to Earth two at a time
Looking for Earthly humans
To take back home
To the dwarf planet or star
What scientists named Pluto years ago
A ball of solid ice and snow
Only with aliens living there
Among the planets them lined
In a straight line from the sun
Their alien brothers and sisters
Of greater command ordered
Them to observe , and prepare a report
Of our Earthlings behavior back
To their home the frozen land
Why are aliens green
This is because cold weather
Can not penetrate
Through their skin
Are there really aliens from Pluto
Living on our Earth
Yes
For if there can be us living on Earth
Then there living somewhere else
There could be them
Why do aliens have an interest in we
Humans of Earth
Maybe they have to study us
For that of a higher power
And a distant land
Above our planet
It is strange for me to see beyond
The smallest planet in the universe

Aliens have lived in my hometown
For several years
They are going now
To explore what is the distance
Of what alien beings were to study
Beyond what we have no knowledge
What is the end of the universe
An alien tea cup powered by unsweetened tea
Can travel as fast as gone and then there
What made it that I could tell this story
It is because
The-two by-two aliens that came to live
Some time on Earth had chosen me
To go with them through space
To their home the planet or dwarf star
Pluto the cold ball of ice and snow
To where to me is a distance unknown
So the green creatures or aliens
With their lightbulb heads
Brought me back to Earth and repowered
Their flying teacup with unsweetened tea
And flew it back into space to their home land
And they were never seen on Earth again

The Music of Halloween

It is time to sing again
With the ghostly
Tumbleweeds
Blowing and Rolling with
The howling wind
The wind chime displaying
Beautiful musical notes
Of peaceful ghostly sounds
A trick-or-treater
Dancing in yesterdays
Garden with the skeletonized
Scarecrow
That Stands somewhat weathered
With the brown corn stalks
Which had become
Fodder Shocks
Listen to the ghostly
Sounds of the
Wind as it whistles
Halloween
With the water rushing producing
The sounds that
Are more ghostly
Than the music
Distributed by the wind
Where does the
Music of the candy bar
Rapper come from
Is it the ghostly
Song of the hand
That plays the violin strings
Or is it those potatoes
Echoing from the
Cold ground
Where has the

Musical choir
That once lived
In this garden
Of yesterday become
Like gardens
They come and go
Just like an
Early Halloween snow
The wheels of the car
Have you ever
Heard them sing
The song of Halloween
The ghost living
Up high in
The old White Oak
Seems to be
Shakey
Rattling the limbs
Of their dwelling
For the musical choir
Everything
On Earth
At one time
Or another
Had played in the
Halloween Musical choir
During
The Past
The present
And the future
Music of Halloween
Sounds and whispers
Of all of the Musical
Choirs of Halloween

You

Here's to you
It takes all
Kinds to make
The world
You lead such
A useless life
You don't contribute
Anything
There are some
Responsibilities
There are just
Too much sometimes to bear
People come to me
And ask me
How to live
I tell them to live is to live
No dog should
Ever waste his time
When he should be out chasing rabbits
I suppose
The first question
That comes to your mind
Why does this job have to be done?
At first I was pretty upset
It was a real emotional blow
All sorts of things
Went through my mind
Don't feel sorry for me
Why, I can see things now
That I never knew
Existed before
You of all People
It would be different
If it were
Someone else

Just a Dream

There wasn't a clue
The Camden-Carroll Library
Reading Room
A camping ground
Librarians, staff, and student workers
Will go
Into the dark deep forest
Just outside the Circulation Desk
Birds and other critters
Sing beautifully within their habitat
Crystal clear water
Trickling down stream
Nature's music
Tree branches creating musical notes
With the howling of the wind
Imagine
Sitting on the bank
Of a creek, river, or lake
Observing fish jumping above
The water from down below
Wondering
If artificial bait
Would be beneficial
For hooking
One of the trophies
Tagged fish----hundred dollar prize
Night crawlers
For catching Blue Channel Cats
After the long mild winter
And the late spring warmth
A camping
And fishing I went
It had been terrific
Even though
I had not a catch

None of the baits
Seemed to Get-R-Done
Let us say Grace
Eat now
Fill your plates
With the camping food
Time
Soon will pass
Rest follows
Tents had been
Assembled
Upon the forest floor
I've never had a dream
So realistic as this before
Camping and fishing
I am in the Reading Room
Inside of the Camden-Carroll Library
Not a forest at all
This is the location
Where students study academically
Without noisy interruptions
This wasn't a dream
For the past two hours
The Reading Room inside
Of the Camden-Carroll Library
Had become the location
For my camping trip
The forest and everything
Within this habitat was real

The Man of Basketball
(How He Defeated Them All)

The man of basketball
A basketball
Player was he
Why did he play
The game so well
Winning was his goal
His team had lost
Their first year
Of playing Basketball
Within the University games
The math team
How they took the court
The trophy
And all of the sport
Watch out for next year
The man of basketball stated
We will play NBA style
He hit the nail
Right on the head
For next year
Did become reality
The math team
And all the other teams
Had become defeated
By the man of basketball
And his basketball
All-stars
Honored he was
And his team and him
Were rewarded
A certificate
And a bowl of soup
After the University games
Had come to an end

The man of basketball and his team
Had not played
Much Basketball since
But dreamed that they had went
To ESPN to play and win
The trophy and the net
From a basketball court
Within the NBA

Sandy

The days of my mountain name
Came and went
So have the days
Of Morehead State
LRC for the past
Three years
The talking of dogs
And Little Tokyo
Rain it did many times
Throughout each year
She a talker
Sure she is
At times buckets of sun
Were plentiful
But during the days
Clouds of gray
There were none
Hard to say for sure
Chemistry is not for me
But I earned the score
Bio Medical
Is my career
One more year
After this one
My undergraduate
Academic program will end
With a Morehead State University
Degree in my hand
What will her
Great friend from
The same mountains
As her do
When all is said and done
For there will not be a bucket
Anywhere else to catch some sun

Comba from the land
Of the mountains
Within Eastern Kentucky
Will be fine
For her favorite dog
Besides the one
Or more she has now
Is Germany's Great Dane
Dogs will come
Dogs will go
Only the ones
She cares for the most
Will steal the show
Wherever her career
Takes her
Will be just fine
For her gaining
Of more knowledge
Will travel
With time
She enjoys
What she makes
Especially
When she bakes
Her friend's favorite
Lemon cake
The two like
Peas in a pod
Larry the Cable Guy
Says Get-R-Done
The other
Says Did-Ya-Now
Who will be
The winner
Of the race
Will it be
The turtle

Or will it be
The Rabbit
The ending
Of a traditional literature tale
Can be somewhat
Of a different outcome
Or can it now
This poem will close
For now
It hard to say
But this
Poem may never come
To an end

The Two Little Hungry Pigs

All five of us have chased
The Two Little Hungry pigs
Being one of blue
The other of red
For several days
But finally
We caught them
And they wanted to make
Their adventurous trip
To the high mountain of Kentucky
To which
They now call their home
These are two of the colors that appear
Within a rainbow
After a warm rain
On a partly cloudy day
During Spring and Summer
The Mother and Aunt did inform me
And I informed
All who became a part
Of the feeding process
Which it took
To feed The Two Little Hungry Pigs
We have all
Heard of the story of The Three Little Pigs
But now a new story
Is in the process of being completed
It is a true story
Of The Two Little Hungry Pigs
That will never be forgotten
And daily fed
Always remember
To share the following words
Everyone can keep
Feeding the little Hungry Pigs

Feed them in such a way
They will never be hungry again
The two Well-Fed Little Pigs
Look well contented
In the nursery
Waiting on their owner's arrival
The Aunt and I are hoping
That the mother will have
Help feeding
Her Son's Two Little Hungry Pigs
For years and years to come
The old saying
Tells us from long ago
That at the end
Of every rainbow
There are
Two Well-Fed Little Pigs
Filled with gold
Being one of Blue
The other of Red
The mother and father
How proud they
Will always be
Of their son
And his Aunt Sandy

Santa's Sleigh Ride Before Christmas

Twas all through Morehead
Not a car was traveling
Snow White upon the ground
Just as sparkling
As frost on Santa's Sleigh
Gas stations
Stores closed
Christmas Eve
Perfect weather
For the job
Of Santa
And his Elf
Tiny Tim
A job to deliver
Presents of all
Makes and kinds
To everyone
Living within our world
Before Christmas Day
At Frosty the Snowman's
Snow Castle
Santa makes a stop
To take this creation
Of snow and ice
With him and his helper
Along for the ride
It is time for
You
The Reader
To finish Writing
This poem

Bluegrass Music of Bill Monroe
And Sarah Kate Morgan

People who had migrated
To America in the 1600s
From Ireland, Scotland, and England
Brought with them
Their Basic styles of music
Which are considered
To be the roots of bluegrass music
That is sung today
As the Jamestown settlers
Began to move
Out into North and South Carolina,
Tennessee, Kentucky, Virginia,
And West Virginia
They wrote songs about day-to-day life
In the new land
The songs reflected life on the farm
Mainly in the mountainous regions
Of the Eastern United States
This genre of music
At its beginning
Was known as mountain music
The invention of the phonograph
And the onset of the radio
In the early 1900s
Brought this music
Out of the rugged mountains
And into the homes of people
Throughout the United States
The Monroe Brothers
Became one of the most popular
Bluegrass Music bands throughout the 1920s
and 1930s
Charlie Monroe played the guitar
Bill Monroe played the mandolin

They sung their songs in harmony
The brothers' band split up in 1938
Each one travelled on
To form their own Independent bands
Bill Monroe was a native of Kentucky
The Bluegrass State
Therefore he named his band
Bill Monroe and the Bluegrass Boys
His band began a new form
Of traditional country music
By the 1950s
People began referring
To this style of music
As Bluegrass Music
Bill Monroe became known
As the Father of Bluegrass Music
O Brother, Where Art Thou
The movie
Assisted with the attraction
Of widening audiences to attend
Bluegrass music shows
Let us travel with the Morehead Band
With the Tradition
Of Bluegrass Music and Dancing
With the Morehead State University
And the Kentucky Center
For Traditional Music
Upstairs on the second floor of the
Old Rowan County Court House
Come inside our doors
You will not leave our
Bluegrass events
Without us teaching you
How to square dance
Sarah Kate Morgan enjoys
Playing this genre of music
Like Bill Monroe

And other Bluegrass Music performers
Before her
The music of Sarah Kate Morgan
Embodies her respect and joy
Of folk music
Backing traditional Appalachian melodies
And singing old time tunes
With fresh harmonies
Of Mountain Music
Accompanying pure and heartfelt vocals
Closely associated with Jean Richie
Of the Mountains within Hazard Kentucky
With the unpretentious sound
Of the Appalachian dulcimer
You can only discover Sarah Kate Morgan
And her dulcimer performances
Of Folk, Americana, and Old-Time roots of
Bluegrass Music
When they are brought
To the forefront of live shows
Like Charlie and Bill Monroe
Carter and Ralph Stanley
Sarah Kate Morgan
Began within the journey
Of Bluegrass Music and Square Dancing
At an early age
How early one might ask
At the age of seven
There will never be an end
To Bluegrass music
Of the olden days
The days of Bluegrass music now
Or the days of Bluegrass music
That is yet to be written and sung
For all to hear

The Bottle Rocket Man

Fire Cracker Dan
Did not have anything
On the Bottle Rocket Man
For Fire Cracker Dan
Had to march to war
With his thousand Soldiers
Dancing Marching Band
Bottle Rocket Man
Would by himself
Fly within the zone of war
And blow himself to pieces
Within enemy lines
When one Bottle Rocket Man
Dies within the field of battle
There is another
Bottle Rocket Man born
To suit up in his
Military uniform
Let him
The Bottle Rocket Man
Do the dances
Of a Thousand bumblebees
Before he becomes
Scattered on the ground